T0198798

Collection of Inspirational Poems for Young Readers

By Annie Peralta

Illustrated By Cariza Bernabe

Inspiring Voices books may be ordered through booksellers or by contacting:

Inspiring Voices
1663 Liberty Drive
Bloomington, IN 47403
www.inspiringvoices.com
1 (866) 697-5313

ISBN: 978-1-4624-0918-1 (sc)
ISBN: 978-1-4624-0919-8 (e)

Printed in the United States of America.

Inspiring Voices rev. date: 2/28/2014

This Book is written to give inspirations to young
readers as well as people of all ages.
To give encouragement to look into
the positive aspect of life with faith and hope.

ABOUT THE AUTHOR

Annie Peralta has been in the immigration business working as an Immigration specialist, Consultant, and Legal Assistant for Inter-World Immigration Service which she owns and manage, serving the international community across America for over 25 years. She possesses a strong background in Immigration law, has written and published various articles on Immigration issues and topics, Los Angeles, California. In her weekly column "A Day in a Life", she has written articles about life, ideas, opinions and many more. Published in the "Who's Who in California" Book, 1986 Edition. Was a professor of English and American Literature, Philippine Women's University and Centro Escolar University. She graduated from the University of Santo Tomas, Manila, Philippines, Faculty of Philosophy and Letters, with a degree in Bachelor of Literature in Journalism. Graduated and finished a Master of Arts degree in Teaching English as a Second Language, University of the Philippines.

ABOUT THE ILLUSTRATOR

Cariza Bernabe is a graduate of California State University, Northridge, in 2008 with a degree in Bachelor of Arts, major in arts with concentration in graphic design and computer animation.. Has excellent ability in illustration, drawing and sketches. Artistic in painting, specializing in landscape and portrait.

Table of Contents

Enjoy Nature's Peace

By Annie Peralta

Enchanting fields, mountain rocks and hills
Exquisite meadows, dancing flowers and daffodils
Flowing rivers, brooks, waterfalls and streams
Are splendorous views offering tranquility and peace.

Beautiful lakes under the clear blue sky
Surrounding trees along countryside
Are all enjoyment to the sight
Drives away solitude and lonely night

Nature's peace heals a burdened heart
Its whispers make worries depart
Life shared with these creations
Finds no reason or room for gloom

The Morning Sun

By Annie Peralta

When the morning sun is up
God already poured unto us
His love, grace and blessing
For our own well being

Prosperity happiness health,
Good luck and authority
He has bestowed on us for free
All you need to do is
Receive it positively

When the morning sun is up
You have all the chances to catch up
And lift up with faith, hope and trust
Put your dreams and goals into action
You have the opportunity all day long

For when the sun sinks down on the bay
It is the end of the day
Hope you didn't miss a single ray
Before shadows of darkness
Shields your pathway

There is Always a Way

By Annie Peralta

Do you feel you have reached the end of your line
And no one else seems treating you so kind
Believe and in faith you stay
For there is always a way

Through your trials and agony
Through your sadness and misery
God is always on the way
To wipe your tears away

For there is always a way
To relieve you in great dismay
To bring that smile back in your day
All you have to do, is to trust, ask and pray

Why I Love the Beach

By Annie Peralta

I go to the beach
Not just to feel the breeze
But to contemplate and listen
To the ocean's gentle murmur
Slow, endless, calm and serene.

I go the beach
Not to swim, wade or play
Just to watch the water
Rejuvenating the soul
In a quiet and peaceful way.

I go to the beach
To thank the powerful hands
That made and designed the ocean,
The grandeur and beauty of the horizon
And the color of the setting sun

God's Wondrous Task

By Annie Peralta

Anxious moments may come to pass
But worry not, it does not last
For God is always on the way
To remove that gloomy day

When I find myself in distress
I always long for His caress
And walk around mountains high
To feel His presence and His smile.

The lakes, the rivers and oceans vast
Are all but God's wondrous tasks
Each day He brings us gift
That our souls may find relief

Four beautiful seasons He created
makes us feel how we are blessed
Just watching God's creations
Reduces my tribulations

All woes and tears of painful heart
In Him we must just cast
Till sunshine paves the way
And sorrows go away

Desires of Your Heart

By Annie Peralta

My beloved child, what is the desire of your heart?
Now that you are growing so fast
Each hour, each moment of your life
Treasure them now, for your
Childhood will not stay here to last
Tomorrow, your today will be yesterday
And your tomorrow will be another day
Cherish all your precious memories
They don't come back again as you grow in years
All your secret dreams and longings
Nobody knows them but Him
May the career, love life and friends
That you have chosen

Brighten your days and undertakings
My dear child, whatever the desires of your heart
Follow them all in the right path
Your daily journey along the road
May be rocky, tough and snowed
If you tumble and cry
With hope rise up again and try
Place all your cares in the Lord's hand
He has endless solution
Beyond your comprehension
Open your heart for He will listen
Always there for you
Never tired of watching

Flower Blessing

By Annie Peralta

The leaves, the vine that climb
Lovely as they relax the mind
The foliage, the shrubs, the buds
Add colors and fragrance divine

Pink, crimson, yellow and green
Spark landscapes and gardens like dream
Give joy and ease the pain
To a weary soul in vain

Sometimes storm winds and heavy rains
Steal their blossoms, roots, and beautiful mornings
So let's join butterflies, bees and birds singing
Let's cheer and smell their fragrance
Before they wither, and leave our senses again

The greatest gift and blessing
Are flowers that bloom in autumn and Spring
Heavenly Father, I praise and thank You
For these precious creations You bring

A Day's Offering

By Annie Peralta

Every day, as you wake up in the morning
Offer to Him first your life, your prayer
Your joys, works and sufferings

Offer your prayer today
To receive favor from His hands
According to His own will and plans

Offer to Him today
Your life with its joy and struggle
That you be guided to find your way
As you continue to strive and to paddle

Offer your works today
May it turn good with His guidance and care
Offer your sufferings today
That your burdens may be lighter and fair

I Am Grateful

By Annie Peralta

I am grateful Lord, for the talent
The intelligence and the wisdom
For happy memories, friends and loved ones
I am grateful for making all things possible
For abundant harvest, a place to stay
And food on the table
I am grateful for life full of blessing
For fresh air, sunshine and rain
For the gift of faith, hope and understanding
I am grateful for showing me the way
When everything is going astray
I am grateful for every new dawning day
For the courage and strength to follow
Your will in every step of the way

Prayer works

By Annie Peralta

Prayer dominates when other means are ineffective
When other approach is powerless
Unravels so many wreckages
Interferes into so many difficulties

Prayer is the means that solves a lot of troubles
Intercedes when you are disturbed
Scared, concerned and perturbed

Worry does not change any situation
But prayer does, when you seek
For solemn divine intervention

So why worry when you can pray
Believe for it works, and expels
All your anxieties away

The Brighter Side

By Annie Peralta

When darkness befalls your path
And clouds of loss, disappointments
And uncertainties overcome you
Go to the brighter side of Life
In there you'll find
Light to brighten your way
Hope to get you out of despair
Grace to bear your trials
Strength to carry your load
Good bounties to sustain your needs
Peace and rest to calm your heart
Energy to give you fresh start
And best of all eternal and undying love
From the righteous hands up above
All these you get when you look
At the brighter side of life.

Take Some Time

By Annie Peralta

Time, as it ticks and moves
No one can interrupt nor hold
Time is an opportunity
That measures longevity

Don't take time for granted
So you don't lose it and wasted
For when it flies and gone
That chance may never come

Take some time to heal wounds
And take time to right wrongs
Take some time to value its worth
And meaning for every pursuit

Take some time to smell the flowers
Along life's circuitous hours
For when beauty and fragrance fades
It is too late for cares and regrets

You Never Know

By Annie Peralta

You never know
What the hours, the days will bring
It can be a fulfillment of a dream
Or a newly born baby awaiting
For a mother's arms caring and loving

Life is what we call an adventure
For you never know what is in store
Always look ahead for a future
That is bright, happy and secure

So discard all thoughts of fear of the unknown
Those are just formed in the imagination
They do not happen
Without the Lord's permission

You never know when the sun will shine
You never know when the sea is calm
You never know when the stars will come
Surely, God knows all that
For He created them all in His hands

Childlike Simplicity

By Annie Peralta

Innocent, pure, simple and trusting
Is what a child's heart
Empty of pride, open to good
Desirous of nothing, undemanding
And always believing
To do good things and please God
You neither need radiance nor beauty
Or intelligence, wealth or popularity
You can give Him, what He wants of you
More innocence and greater childlike simplicity

Voices and Sights of Summer

By Annie Peralta

Summer is the time when
The beach comes to life
With endless laughter and frolic
Of small children and parents alike

Voices fill the air of beach water
With people feeling the warmth of the sun
Sunbathing or building castle
All done in the sand

Couples rollerblading, biking
Kite flying or volleyball playing
Enjoyment and merrymaking
Are all sights of summer fun

Summer is the time when
Campground is crowded with tents
Campers, families, and friends
Relaxing, gathering, sharing
Outdoor dining and laughing

Summer is the time to take a glimpse
at flower gardens, rich in beauty and green
Worries and concerns are forgotten
When summer's gentle flowing breeze
Touches the face with soft caress

Laughter the Free Medicine

By Annie Peralta

Just like the wind and the sun
Laughter is your freedom
For mind, body and soul
Laughter is the greatest medicine of all

Laughter raises positive feelings
Vanishes anxiety, anger and pain
As your hours and days are shortened
Laugh and for sure it will be lengthened

Let not problems fill your eyes with tears
Laughing stimulates hopes,
Relieves burdens and fears
Has powerful way to boost energy and vitality
And most of all it is free

Beauties of Fall

By Annie Peralta

Petals sprinkled by showers of dawn
Kissed by early sunshine in the morn
Rare beauties on the ground
Delights butterflies roaming around

Autumn leaves falling like cascading water
Are nature's symphony and rhythm every where
Admiring these beauties of fall
Makes us closer to our creator

Varieties of coloring trees on walkways
Removes cares, inspires our days
Violets, gold, blue and canary
Are all God's treasured colors
Made for us to see

The Two Roads

By Annie Peralta

Wide and broad, that's one of the roads
Hectic, happy- go- lucky, trendy,
The way of the world
Heavily traveled by the majority
Because it is fast and easy
Lack in faith, and values
In principles, and moral virtues
Leads to destruction, no destination

Narrow is the other road
difficult, restricted not easy
not popular, traveled by few
not the way of the crowd
the way to the Lord

Our life is like a road
Take the narrow road
And you obey the Lord
Take the wide road
You abandon the way of the Lord

Leave It in His Hands

By Annie Peralta

You struggled, exhausted and defeated
Drenched with sorrow, depressed and isolated
Let go of your problems and trouble
Your tensions, conflicts and rubbles
Leave it all in His mighty hands

In His hands, no task is tedious and hard
Always ready to preserve and guard
No burden is heavy to carry
For love of you, He can
Do it all without weary

In His hands though your battle is tough
He will fight and uphold you to the last
In times of adversity
His hands will carry you to safety

Rely in His divine power
His kingdom can all conquer
Be not afraid but take courage
When your life is in His hands
Nothing surpasses His commands

Calm and Relaxed

By Annie Peralta

Make life slow, relax and easy
Calm and quiet as the waves of the sea
Release those anger, hatred and unhappiness
Remorse, frustration and bitterness
Find rest for your tired soul
By meditation worship and communion
Shift your eyes from self-pity to victory
From negative to blessed
Remain calm and confident
When terrifying thoughts assail you
In quietness, rest in Him in assurance
And peace He will give you

Humility

By Annie Peralta

Humility is when the heart is void with
Selfishness, arrogance and conceit
When it is humble, collected, simple and content
Not pompous, boastful of wealth and achievement
Humility is when you are kind, lenient and mild
In your language, thoughts and actions
Humility is when you yield
Your egotistical superiority and pride
When you place yourself last in line
And concede without any whine
Humble yourself when you pray
In all humility He inclines
His ear to every word you say

My Changeless Friend

By Annie Peralta

In times of distress and weariness
I go to Him, my changeless Friend
He comforts me, consoles and enlightens
When others reject or fail me
When my hands cannot work
And I am alone and gloomy
He is always there to assist me

In spite of my faults, weaknesses of any kind
He is changeless, always willing to
Accept me any time
You too can go to Him
He is waiting for you to be His friend
Believe for He is most powerful
He will walk you from sorrow and pain

Patience

By Annie Peralta

Patience is the key that opens the door
To so many wishes, dreams and galore
Patience is a fulfillment of something new
Always remember it as a wonderful virtue

Practice patience all around
In churches, homes, and school grounds
In gardening, workplaces all sorrounds
And reap happiness, success, and joy with a crown

Let nothing upsets or stops you
Let not delays, holds and troubles bother you
Replace impatience and anger with a prayer
For He knows what load you bear
In patience, in His will, you'll receive your share

It Will Pass

By Annie Peralta

I may not know what's troubling you
Only One knows for sure
What you're going through
Whatever it is, in Him you entrust
He will bring it to pass

He does not promise to deliver you
From hardship, turmoil and pain
But He promises to stay with you
Throughout, the course
Of your problem and suffering

He does not give you a burden
Beyond your strength and understanding
Or any load, anguish or misery
Heavier than you can carry

He reveals how to get out of your agony
He supplies you with grace and mercy
Never stop praying and asking
No matter how hopeless it may seem
Whatever you are undergoing
It will pass, just commit in Him

Can't Buy Everything

By Annie Peralta

Just when you think money has wings
That can fly you everywhere you dream
Pause and realize it can't buy everything
It will only take you to the extreme

When age sets in, can't buy youth
And good looks, an undeniable truth
When health deteriorates
Can't buy it with money
To recover strength, stamina, vitality

Can't buy happiness to fill the emptiness
Can't buy peace of mind
When the heart is restless
Complete package for mental health
Enough necessities less worries

Acquisitive compulsion not worth the gamble
Money, risky stake and materialistic venture
Can't take it with you with all its trouble
When your time is up to depart the earth after all

On Winter Mornings

By Annie Peralta

The morning fog, the chilly wind
Are scenes of winter morning
On winter morning, I find myself watching
Snowflakes on my windows gently falling

On winter morning, I find myself again dreaming
Of going to the mountain and enjoy the fun of skiing
On winter morning, I gaze at
White grounds filled with children
Throwing snowballs playing and merrymaking
All these moments come alive, only on winter mornings.

The Real Treasure

By Annie Peralta

Precious gems, jewels, expensive things and possessions
Material acquisition with burning desire and ambition
Lives with superficial glitter and illusions
Are but worldly treasures
Not worth to keep and store
On earth decay destroys them
And can also be stolen

Think of the sick, the hungry and the needy
The lonely, the depressed and helpless
Share love, care and attention
For where your heart is
The real treasure in heaven will be.

Just Move on

By Annie Peralta

Just move on, though
You are in disgrace and in tears
Keep moving, keep going,
He will shelter you from fears
And strengthen you to forbear

Don't attempt on anything
Damaging to the soul and brain
Sinful digression, just to escape the pain
Intolerable, excruciating the situation you're in

Don't be frustrated or despondent
Move on, do your best today
You'll find your spirit
Renewing on the way

He keeps His eyes on
Whatever you do, wherever you go
There is a bright hope for tomorrow
For His powerful presence is always with you

I Don't Mind

By Annie Peralta

It may be raining today
But I don't mind
For sunshine is on the way
The day may have some sorrow
Yet I don't mind
For there is tomorrow

Dreams may be hard to follow
Still I don't mind
Hope dwells not in a hollow
Good old friends may be gone
But I don't mind
New ones are here to come

Some stairs are hard to climb
But I don't mind
Rewards are waiting behind
So why should I mind
If life sometimes doesn't seem all right
I know Someone great up in the sky
Is making all things wonderful and bright.

The Christmas Star

By Annie Peralta

The night the little precious child is born
Heaven shared its bright star
To shine its light from afar
And bring high hope, happiness and joy
For all forlorn hearts laden with sorrow

The Christmas star invites the world
To come and give honor to our Lord
Laid in a manger, asleep and cold
Wrapped in swaddling clothes

Peace and all our dreams on earth
We will receive through His Birth
Let's follow the star and forget our cares
To our savior all we can offer
Homage, worship, praises and prayer

Printed in the United States
By Bookmasters